PSYCHOLOGY OF CONFIDENCE

ARVIND UPADHYAY

Made with ♥ on the Notion Press Platform
www.notionpress.com

Only a few human characteristics have enough power to set people apart. With such qualities, you can conquer the world; without them, you get stuck and don't make much progress. Confidence tops the list of these characteristics. When you have confidence, you can do almost everything; interact with people, talk to them, work on projects, write books, play your favorite sport, sing your favorite song in public, get things done. In short, you can move through the world without worrying about getting socially accepted. And this is exactly what this book can help you achieve. With this book, I want to provide my readers with the tools and techniques they can use to not only gain confidence but also to avoid the destructive thoughts. The discussed confidence-building techniques are of great value to people belonging to all walks of life. I hope that this book inspires you and gives you the confidence you've been looking for. Start off to take the first step toward confidence improvement.

Contents

1

what if I could be more confident

Are you eager to try some exciting things, but then lose the courage? Are you delaying completing that picture, writing that book, setting up a new business, or expressing your inner feelings to that special person in your life? Did you hesitate to answer these questions? Or was your immediate answer a YES? Regardless of the situation, you are lacking the confidence to take the initiative. To tell you the truth, most people fail to understand the real meaning of the term confidence. And that is why they don't experience the confidence that can turn their lives around. Continue reading to find out how you can break free from those unhealthy habits that don't let you move forward. What Confidence Really is Most people think that confidence means realizing your ability to do things well. For instance, you might find someone saying, "I'm a writer, and I have confidence in my ability to write on any topic, to be able to create interesting characters and situations," and so on. Or, "I'm an educated person, and I have confidence in my ability to secure a well-paid job, to be able to get a promotion, and to lead my subordinates." So what's the problem with such beliefs? Well, they make you feel that you have to do something, such as writing, painting, leading, or earn a lot of money to become confident. This simply means that your confidence is based on the things that you can do well. As a result, you tend to feel confident at certain times – when you're doing that particular task. That means that if you write books and you do it well, you can feel confident during the moment you write an article or book, but the rest of the time, you simply won't. This is how most people restrict the amount of time they can feel confident. This further explains why a huge number of individuals become obsessed with certain activities. After all, they feel confident about themselves only when they're doing that task, job, or simply utilizing their ability. It is important to understand that confidence doesn't have anything to do with what happens in your life. True confidence doesn't come from outside. Instead, it is developed from within. It originates from a promise you make to your own self – a promise that you will achieve whatever you need to achieve in life. The foundation of confidence is based on the trust you have in yourself, not in the results you may or may not achieve. No matter how much you acquire or accomplish in life, if you can't find enough confidence within, then all those external successes or achievements simply don't mean anything. In short, true confidence is the belief you have in your own spirit – that regardless of your circumstances, you will face every obstacle or difficulty to achieve your aim. It doesn't represent your actions to achieve a certain target; it reflects your willingness to act.

What Confidence is not

Confidence represents different things to different people. Similarly, it evokes different feelings and reactions within people. While it is easy to understand what confidence really means, it is even easier to associate it with certain negative emotions and human responses. And that's why it is imperative to define the terms that are often wrongly linked with confidence so we are all on the same page and understand what we're talking about.

Confidence vs. Overconfidence

Overconfidence is such a strange psychological defense that it is sometimes difficult to separate it from confidence. But remember that they definitely are not the same thing. Let's say you have to deliver a speech on an unfamiliar topic. If you act after understanding your limitations and realizing your chances of failure, you're confident. You are aware of your weaknesses, understand that you should make necessary preparations before going for the speech, and accept all the possible outcomes; it is called confidence. Overconfidence comes into situation when you ignore all chances of failure. You realize that you can't deliver an impromptu speech, but you still don't prepare beforehand and ignore even the slightest chance of failure. In situations like these, you act like an overconfident person. This usually happens when your beliefs or feelings exceed your capabilities. Such people tend to underestimate the risks to which they are vulnerable.

Confidence vs. Arrogance

Though arrogance is an entirely different attitude, it is often mistaken for confidence. Arrogance is basically the notion of being confident with an inclination toward bragging, showing off, elitism, etc. Have you ever seen those people with a heavy body, overdeveloped muscles and who push their chests out intentionally and walk pompously? Such individuals represent arrogance, and not confidence. The reason being confidence originates from within and when you're truly confident, you don't need to demonstrate it to the world. Have you ever seen Arnold Schwarzenegger, Sylvester Stallone, or Dwayne Johnson swaggering around? Of course not. They have a powerful yet quiet confidence that doesn't need any proclamation. A truly confident person doesn't have to brag about his/her achievements. Those who brag only try to mask their insecurities about themselves. If your confidence comes from within, you'll let your achievements speak for themselves. On the other hand, if someone continuously broadcasts his/her confidence, they are actually trying to convince others as well as themselves. In fact, they are using an ineffective technique to gain confidence.

Confidence vs. Belligerence

You might have seen some people exhibiting certain "bad boy" characteristics. Many of us perceive such traits as confidence. This confidence is just an excuse for a super-violent attitude. This doesn't mean that you shouldn't asset yourself when needed. But confidence doesn't mean that you can bully people or trample over them either. A person is belligerent when he/she is aggressive, abrasive, and insensitive to the relationships he has with others. True confidence, on the other hand, enables you to lead your life happily without having a negative impact on those around you. Confidence helps you learn how you can make others feel good only because you can

Significance of Confidence

Let's get down to why confidence matters in our daily life. Well, confidence is important because it is the only thing that makes the most difference. Sounds difficult? When individuals continually struggle, move towards their goals, and make the right adjustments, they have better chances to get great results and reach their targets. Nevertheless, if they don't have that same confidence, they tend to get stuck. It is almost as if they don't have any goals or dreams at all. Having true confidence, particularly in the context of working to achieve your objectives, is absolutely essential. After all, lack of confidence can impede your progress and keep you from pursuing your dreams. A great part of your achievements depends on how confident you are.

2
Relationship between Capability and Confidence

Is a capable person a confident person? Not, not necessarily. In fact, capability and confidence represent two distinct concepts, so understanding their essentials is important. While capability denotes your capacity to do or achieve something, confidence shows your belief about your capability. Every individual has his/her own beliefs, values, and experiences that enable them to perceive life in their own unique way. They have their own opinions about reality. The amazing part of this notion is that these opinions and views can be changed and thus change one's idea of life. This implies that the strategies and exercises discussed in this book have the ability to alter your perception of what you can achieve.

Capability without Confidence

What happens when a person has a capability but lacks confidence? Well, they get stuck and don't make any progress. They might understand some of the most complex concepts perfectly, but are never able to implement them. A person who has the knowledge and capability to achieve something and does nothing is not much different from someone who doesn't know anything and is incompetent. Always remember that action is the real fruit of knowledge. It is only your fear of the unknown and lack of confidence that holds you back from achieving your goals. The following key beliefs can enable you to move forward and take the right action: You are a creative person. You know everything to take the first step. If you don't know something right now, you'll learn it or find someone to help you out eventually. Aren't these beliefs empowering and relieving? It is quite not possible for anyone to know everything before starting on any project. Once you understand the difference between an empowering behavior and a stuck behavior, you'll naturally discern any times that you might get stuck. And in that situation, you simply need to adjust your attitude and keep moving forward.

Confidence without Capability

People who lack capability but have baseless confidence tend to become a complete disaster. Here's an example: a person has never driven a car before, but think he/she is an ace driver because they read a book on driving a few years ago. Would you let that person drive the car while you sit in the passenger seat? The answer is obvious. Confidence without capability is dangerous not only for concerned individuals but also for those around them.

Capability + Confidence

When capability and confidence combine in a person, virtually nothing can stop him/her from becoming successful. They have all the tools and techniques they need to achieve their dreams. They are unstoppable. So they just go for their goals. This is the peak of success. When you have these two characteristics combined, nothing can or will stop you from moving forward. This is when you realize that any obstacle or difficulty that you face is just an opportunity in disguise that highlights your resourcefulness. The following points summarize the basic success formula: You define an objective. You closely observe the results you get. You adjust your approach until you achieve the desired objective. Setting an objective indicates that you have a vision of what you aim for. When you know what you want to achieve, you can accomplish it more easily. Observing your results indicates that you have the sensory insight to identify what works for you and what doesn't. When something works for you, you use it more often and in a much better way. And when something doesn't give you the desired results, you ask yourself how you can do it differently to get better results. Adjusting your approach simply means that you persevere and continue doing things differently, trying different techniques, and using a variety of strategies until you achieve your desired outcome. Follow this success formula, and you'll soon find yourself meeting and going beyond all your expectations.

3

The Basics of Self-Confidence

Can you tell the difference between high and low self-confidence? Well, it's quite simple. People who describe themselves, their accomplishments, relationships, and all other associations in a negative way, they may have low self-confidence. Yes, we all do some of that at some time in our life, but only people with low self-confidence think like that on a regular basis. By low self-confidence, we simply mean that such people generally have a negative overall view of their abilities, judge and evaluate their achievements negatively, and criticize themselves. They have a negative, rigid belief about others as well as themselves. These opinions are sometimes taken as facts or truths about themselves that ultimately cause a negative impact on their personalities and lives.

Though the views you have about yourself may seem to be factual statements, they are actually only opinions. The truth is the experiences you've had in life form your opinions. These experiences further let you understand your nature and personality. If you've had negative experiences, your views about yourself tend to be negative as well. Crucial experiences that develop our views about ourselves usually, but not always, happen early in life. What you see, hear, and experience in the childhood days have a great impact on the way you view yourself. Many times, negative opinions about yourself can also be caused by experiences you have in later life. For instance, workplace intimidation or bullying, persistent hardship or stress, traumatic events, or abusive relations are also a cause of low self-discipline among people. A few examples of negative experiences that can eventually lead to the development of low self-confidence are discussed below: Rejection Low self-confidence can develop when a person feels rejects by family, friends, colleagues, teachers, etc. Being Bullied If a person is bullied or made fun of in childhood, he/she may develop thoughts like, "I'm stupid," "I'm just not good enough". Being Expected to Meet High Standards A person who is always trying to meet someone else's standards or expectations is likely to develop low self-confidence. Constant criticism from parents, peers, colleagues, or other people can also lead to this negative feeling. Feeling Different From Other People Many people feel that don't fit in, particularly during childhood and adolescence. This has a serious effect on the way they view themselves. At this time, physical appearance is very important to most people. Thoughts like, "people don't like me because I don't look good," or "I'm not good-looking enough" can become real opinions that can ultimately become rigid as they get older. Absence of Positives People who grow up in an atmosphere with a lack of encouragement, affection, warmth, or praise usually lack confidence. For instance, if a kid's basic needs were met, but his/her parents did not show affection physically or emotionally, then the kid can grow up to be a less confident individual. Distressing Life Events People who experience traumatic or stressful events become angry towards others. They may also respond negatively. Relationship breakups, bereavement, or health issues are a few factors that can have an adverse effect on self- confidence. Abuse, Abandonment or Punishment If a kid is unfairly neglected, abused or punished, they may think negatively about themselves. The same is true for those adults who may be in abusive relationships.

Personal Effects of Low Self-Confidence

Low self-confidence can severely influence the way people see themselves, their abilities and talents. This further affects the way they function in their daily life. Some of the possible effects of low self-confidence on the personality of an individual are discussed below: They may say a lot of discouraging things about themselves. They find it difficult to accept compliments. They feel guilty, anxious, frustrated, ashamed, or depressed. They criticize themselves and their abilities and actions. They always think that things can never turn out well for them. They doubt or blame themselves and put themselves down. Their main focus is on the mistakes they made or achievements they couldn't make. They are never able to recognize their positive characteristics.

Effects on Daily Life

The aforementioned personal effects further have a severe impact on their everyday life. Read through the following list to discover how a person with low self-confidence operates in their daily life: Inefficient performance at work. Their fear of failure makes them avoid challenging situations. Since they have a negative opinion of their own abilities, they don't reach their full potential. They believe that their previous achievements are a result of luck rather than their own qualities or abilities. Their relationships with family, friends, or colleagues also get affected. For instance, they may try to please others, avoid social interaction, become extremely self-conscious or shy, or become overly distressed or upset by any disapproval or criticism. A significant change in their appearance can also be observed. While some people lacking self-confidence don't pay much attention to personal care, others try to mask their perceived weaknesses by paying great attention to their looks. The latter may not even look directly in other people's eyes if they think they're not looking perfect. Low self-confidence also has a great impact on their food or alcohol consumption. While some people may go on a severe diet, others may start eating too much. Many people try to find their refuge in alcohol and use harmful drugs as a means to raise their confidence. This, in turn, not only affects their health, but also has an adverse impact on their self-confidence.

Aspects of Low Self-Confidence

Negative opinions and views about yourself can have a damaging effect on your thinking as well as your behavior. This can further affect the way you feel both physically and emotionally. Low self-confidence may have an impact on you as a person in several ways. Different people have different responses to low self-confidence. Some people might have more physical effects, while others might observe negative thinking patterns. Many individuals observe a malicious cycle of symptoms, but not everyone has the same experience. Thoughts and Views You might think you're not good enough for others. You might think that others see you negatively. You might doubt your capabilities and talents. You might blame yourself for everything that happens to you. You might become extremely critical. You might focus on mistakes more than strengths and success. Moods The following list shows some of the most common moods you can observe in any person with low self-confidence: Shame Guilt Anxiety Anger and frustration Sadness Behaviors Rejecting something is extremely difficult for someone with low selfconfidence. They are unable to communicate their needs. They are always trying to make others satisfied, and that's why they are unable to meet their own needs. They are unable to make critical decisions. They hold back from making things happen or avoid challenges. They are shy and avoid meeting and interacting with new people. They are oversensitive. Physical Reactions The following list shows some of the most common physical reactions you can observe in any person with low self-confidence: Tension Tiredness Fatigue Appetite changes Sleep issues.

4

Signs of Great Confidence

By now, you know self-confidence is the way you think and feel about yourself. This single characteristic has enough power to impact almost all aspects of your life, particularly your relationships. If you are self-assured and confident, you tend to find healthier and more positive relationships. Nonetheless, if your confidence level is low, you might put up with something as negative as violence or bullying in a relationship. Confidence is a broad term. Since it is so personal in nature, it is a bit difficult to define it. For most people, confidence is the belief you have in yourself, another individual, or an idea. A confident person shows that they have faith in their personal strength, abilities, and talents. The best thing about confidence is that it doesn't involve any official measure; you are confident as long as you feel confident. A major part of confidence is linked with self-esteem. Individuals with great self-esteem are usually more confident. People with high confidence levels usually feel positive about their ability to progress, take action, and participate. They are happy with their attitudes, behaviors, and overall personalities. Confidence doesn't mean same for every individual. Though different people have different confidence levels, there are some basic signs that are enough to identify a confident person. And with these signs, you can also learn about the origin of confidence. Some common signs of a confident person are that they are always ready to do what they believe to be right. They don't care if it is unpopular among their peers. They are willing to take risks, but they strive to make planned moves. Confident people never hesitate to admit their mistakes and always learn from them. They are optimistic, accept compliments, and treat others with respect. If you don't know how to identify confidence, here a few basic signs and a description of how they make a person feel. Sign: Positivity

How it Feels: They have a good opinion of themselves as well as others. Sign: Sense of self-respect How it Feels: They believe they are important and deserve to be treated with respect. Sign: Encouragement and support for others How it Feels: They nurture and support their family and friends in all their activities. They do not let anyone degrade their loved ones. In fact, they make positive contributions to their relationships and the overall environment. Sign: Healthy communication How it Feels: They understand how they should ask for the things they need and want. Also, they listen to others and respond carefully. Sign: Active participation How it Feels: They try out new hobbies and participate in team activities. They know they can't perform well all the time, but that's perfectly fine with them. Sign: Constant energy How it Feels: They try new, exciting things, physical activities, and exercise routines. Their energy keeps everyone around them energetic and active. Sign: Ability to learn from mistakes How it Feels: Like every other human, confident people also make mistakes. What makes them different is that they use mistakes as learning opportunities so they don't repeat them. Sign: Ambition How it Feels: They always have constructive ideas for their future. Their ambition gives them the motivation to set and work for new and more interesting goals. Since you are now able to identify a confident person, it is equally important to know the signs of low confidence. People with low levels of confidence can be extremely critical of their abilities or personalities. They usually view themselves negatively and think others don't have a good opinion about them. They mostly find it difficult to interact with peers and friends. The following account will further help you identify the basic signs of low confidence: Sign: Self-doubt How it Feels: They don't feel important and think that people don't like them much. Sign: Nervousness How it Feels: They find it really difficult to talk to anyone in a social situation. They are unable to make eye contact or speak in public without any fear. Sign: Anxiousness How it Feels: They feel anxious most of the time and get worried about petty things. Sign: Over-sensitivity How it Feels: They think that people always criticize them and say or do negative things to them. Sign: Doubtfulness How it Feels: They don't trust other people, including their family, friends, peers, or colleagues. They think others will cheat or exploit them. Sign: Negativity How it Feels: They mostly see the glass half empty rather than half full. Sign: Discontent How it Feels: They don't feel happy or satisfied with their work, activities, relationships, or their overall personality. Sign: Hopelessness How it Feels: They are pretty hopeless about everything in their life. Sign: Loneliness How it Feels: They feel lonely a lot of the time and think they don't have anyone they can share their feelings with. Sign: Fear How it Feels: They are scared of trying new things.

Traits of Confident People When it comes to confidence, you can be certain of one thing: confident people are always ahead of the skittish and the doubtful because they encourage others and make things happen. Your mindset has a great impact on your capability to succeed. It is clearly important to be confident, but what sets confident individuals apart from everyone else? In this section, some extraordinary behaviors of truly confident people are uncovered. So read on. Happiness From Within Happiness is one of the most critical aspects of confidence. If you want to be confident in what you achieve, it is necessary to be satisfied with who you are. Confident individuals take their sense of satisfaction and pleasure from their own achievements. They don't care what others think of their accomplishments. They understand that no matter what others say, they are not as good or as bad as people think they are. Avoid Judging Others This is one basic trait that only confident people possess. They avoid passing judgments on the people around them because they understand that everyone has his/her own specialties. They don't try to degrade others so as to feel better about themselves. Another fact that they know is that comparing their abilities with those of others will only limit them. They don't waste their time wondering if they live up to others' expectations or not. Listen to Their Inner Self According to a research conducted by the University of California, the more difficult it is for you to say no to something, the more stressed and depressed you might feel. Confident individuals know that refusing something they don't want is healthy. Their self-esteem enables them to make clear refusals. When it's time to refuse or reject something, confident individuals don't use phrases like "I'm not sure if I can" or "I want to, but I'm not certain." They refuse clearly and openly because they realize that saying no to something they don't need gives them a unique opportunity to fulfill their existing commitments. Listen First, Speak Later People with high levels of confidence give more importance to listening than speaking. They speak less because they don't have the urge to prove anything to others. They believe that they have better chances to grow and prosper by listening and observing others. They don't see interactions as mere opportunities to prove their worth to others. Instead, their main focus is on the communication itself. They make every possible effort to make the interaction more productive and enjoyable. Certainty Matters You might not have seen any confident person uttering phrases like, "I think" or "Um." The reason being they think and then speak assertively. They realize that people don't find you trustworthy or reliable if you're not sure about your ideas or opinions. That is why they make sure to deliver their views with conviction. Enjoy Every Victory Confident people seek out every victory. They challenge themselves, compete, put in the best effort, and then celebrate every small victory. When you enjoy a victory, your brain develops new androgen receptors that further keep it motivated. The increased androgen receptor levels have a positive effect on testosterone, which ultimately boosts their confidence and enable them to tackle more challenges. A series of victories, no matter how small, can keep you motivated for months. Not Desperate for Attention Nobody appreciates people who are just desperate for attention. When it comes to confident individuals, they realize that being yourself is important as people are attracted to the right behavior. They are experts at diffusing attention. If they are given attention for an achievement, they try to shift the focus quickly to others who helped them get there. In short, they don't yearn for the praise or approval because their self-worth originates from within. Accept Their Mistakes Confident individuals never hesitate to accept their mistakes. They put their belief out there to check if it holds up. They learn from others if they are wrong and help others learn from them if they are right. Ask for Help Confident people realize that asking others for help does not make them appear foolish or weak. They understand their strengths and weaknesses and do not hesitate to look to their friends to fill the gaps. They are always willing to learn from someone with more knowledge or expertise. Celebrate Others Confident individuals focus outward which enables them to see and enjoy all of the amazing characteristics of other people. Unlike insecure people, they don't try to be in the spotlight at all times or criticize others just to prove their worth. They praise and appreciate people and make them feel good about their abilities and strengths.

5

The Root Cause of a Lack of Confidence

While several areas are responsible for causing a lack of confidence among people, a few top areas are the media, parents, and educational institutions. We'll see how this happens and also discuss how it is possible to prevent this from happening to your loved ones or even yourself. With the methodology we'll explain later in the book, you can install irresistible confidence in them. In several ways, our society teaches people to "accept what you get" or to "just go with the flow". In most situations, many falsely translate these as suggestions to NOT pursue their dreams. What you should remember is that if you want to step outside the box and go beyond what is considered "normal", then you should do exactly that – follow your dreams.

Parents Many parents can become a major contributor to their children's lack of confidence. While most parents teach their kids to utilize their full potential and help them become what they want to be, some just strip away the kid's uniqueness and unintentionally install limits in them. The latter often, deliberately or inadvertently, try to get their children accept and comply with their own thoughts and opinions. How many times have you seen a parent using any of the following phrases? Act your age Don't act childish Be practical Why are you such a dreamer? How can you say such a silly thing? No one does that except you Grow up Yes, parents want to encourage their child's behavior, but sometimes they are not able to communicate that message positively. For instance, what does the phrase "Grow up" really mean? To restrict yourself as most adults do, to not experience pure happiness like other children, to not wonder, explore, or learn? If that is what "grow up" means, you should pass. Let's take the phrase, "Don't act childish". The idea of learning, enjoying, and exploring is what life teaches us about and kids understand it better than most people. What about the idea of being "practical"? How precisely can one be practical? Calling kids a dreamer or asking them to get real does not help. It only defines limits for them and creates boundaries that are socially acceptable. Educational Institutes After parents, educational institutes are the next big contributors to confidence or its absence. One factor that has a huge impact on confidence is peer pressure. Kids bully each other if someone does something differently. Another unfortunate thing is that most schools divide children into varied learning tracks. For instance, you may find low, medium, and high math or science learners in some schools. Children are smarter and much more intelligent than we think they are. They not only understand such tags but also make them a part of their identities and personalities. The students tagged "slow" add this into their thinking as a belief, "I can't perform well in science." This belief does not just impact their educational excellence, but their overall personality also gets tarnished. In fact, it develops their reality. The top achievers perform according to their expectations. The average ones perform moderately. And the poor performers get poor results. In short, they all perform exactly how they are taught and expected to perform. Beliefs and expectations create reality. Excellence can be expected from anyone. It is important to project positive expectations onto your children. Once done, you'll be surprised to see how people, kids in particular, rise up to the standards defined for them. The Media Lack of confidence also comes from the media. Mainstream media gets its funding from advertising, and that's why it is out to make people consume. Companies invest huge amounts of money showing their products and/or services to the target audience. Your uniqueness is a risky factor for these advertisers. The reason being when you're in a position to think for yourself, you can make a decision regarding the offered product/ service. In such a situation, you don't buy just to conform to the society. Your lack of confidence produces great results for advertisers. They use a plethora of techniques and tactics to strip away your confidence. For instance, they show how every popular celebrity uses their product or service, and therefore you should also use it to become famous, beautiful, wealthy, happy. They make every possible effort to make you feel bad about yourself if you don't use their product. They communicate that your life can get unlimited happiness if you start consuming their products. Have you ever noticed what they show in a typical beer commercial? A skinny guy with a beer is watching TV. What happens next – life becomes an amazing party, he has beautiful women around him, he has a fancy car, he is relaxing on a serene island, and he has no worries at all. And that is how the media teaches you to depend on certain products to live your life to the fullest.

6

Building Confidence

Let me tell you a secret. Confidence is not an entity. It is not something that you can inject into yourself. You can only act confident or behave in a confident manner. And that is why you won't find a pill in the market that can boost your confidence. If you behave in a confident way, you have confidence. On the other hand, if you behave in an uncertain way, you lack confidence. What's more, confidence is not persistent in different facets. So what confidence actually is? Well, it is just a process that you perform inside your mind. The same is true for your emotions, such as anxiety, depressions, fear, or sadness. Not one of these emotions is a real thing. They occur as a result of different processes – series of thoughts that exist in your mind. Once you understand that all this happens in your mind, one of the most important things is to realize that it is possible to control these processes. Only you can determine which mental process is useful to you and which isn't, and then you can interrupt, stop, or banish the negative ones. Give yourself a pat on the back when you stop a negative process successfully or begin a confident process. This is important as you get what you emphasize. Appreciating yourself provides you with an incentive to continue the resourceful process. You'll then automatically do it again, in a better manner, in the future. Make sure to treat yourself well. Many people have discouraging internal voices harassing them all day. Can you imagine how horrible it must be to live hearing those voices? Always remember that you are the one who needs your maximum time and support. Have a great relationship with your own self. Respect yourself. Appreciate yourself. Acknowledge your accomplishments. Congratulate yourself whenever you go beyond your comfort zone. Enjoy your victories and success and reward yourself.

Let Go of the Past Do you often think about your past? Do you wonder why you were shy or less confident or why you could not act in a certain way? Buy why do you think about the time that has already passed? The past is gone. You can't do anything to change it. But yes, you can learn from it and avoid repeating the same mistakes. You can change your behavior in the light of your former attitude. So just forgive your former self for its shyness and lack of confidence. A huge number of people waste their precious time and energy regretting for the time and opportunities they couldn't avail only because of their reluctance to try new things. If you were not confident in the past or were shy or reluctant, it's time to forgive yourself. Let all those negative feelings or frustration go, because they belong to the past. You just need to learn from it and then move on. Practice all those exercises that we'll be discussing in the next few chapters and discover your brand-new confidence. And then if people define you as nervous or shy, you might want to swiftly but respectfully correct them. Go ahead, tell them that, "Yes, I used to be shy in the past. But now I've learned to stay confident in all situations". It will not only convey the message that old limits are not applicable to you anymore, but people will also welcome your new, confident self.

Learn the Language If you listen to yourself and others carefully, you will observe that the vocabulary of confident people is entirely different from those who lack confidence. A vast majority of people speak reflexively, so they usually don't give it a much purposeful thought. Per se, these routine language patterns signify an individual's mindset. In addition to reflecting an individual's mindset, language emphasizes his/her thinking. This implies that by changing your language, you can emphasize new thinking patterns and start seeing a new perspective. The more you do this, the more confident you'll become. The key is to integrate positive vocabulary into your daily life. With the right vocabulary, you change not only your mindset, but also your overall life. So what is positive vocabulary? There are two different types of words. When you integrate the first type of words into your vocabulary, you increase your chances of becoming more confident. However, the elimination of the second type of words from your vocabulary help you reach your ultimate destination. More of these words will be discussed in the next section. For now, let's see how a small change in your language can help you interrupt or even banish negative thought processes. Let's say you've always feared to write. How do you describe this fear to yourself? If you say, "I can't write well because I'm scared of putting my thoughts on paper," you, in a sense, take possession of a negative mental process.

Can you explain what actually happens inside your mind? Well, when you think about a certain action, your mind runs a process that you label as fear. And when you understand this sequence of events, you'll certainly feel better realizing that what you initially considered "a fear of writing" is just a mental process. Try describing other such negative emotions. Observe if you say things like, "I can't talk to strangers because they make me nervous," or "I can't go out because I'm depressed." Instead of saying, "I feel scared", explain for yourself what is actually happening; "My current thinking pattern is making me feel scared". It may sound a little complex at first, but as you practice this technique, it not only makes sense but will also enable you to feel free. So change your life by adding the right phrases in your vocabulary.

Know the Killer Words As discussed in the previous section, two set of words have a strong impact on your life and personality. So let's take a look at the set of words that you need to eliminate from your vocabulary. If you ever find yourself saying any of the following words, remind yourself, "Hey, I'm acting like my old, less confident self. I'm not shy anymore. I have confidence and therefore, I behave confidently. I'm going to use a better vocabulary". But don't beat yourself. Simply accept the fact that you use negative phrases, and then eliminate them from your vocabulary. Hope The first word that you might not see any confident person using is "hope". Yes, hope is a wonderful thing that you should have in life, but it inevitably presumes a lack of action. Phrases like "I just hope things get better eventually," or "I hope they understand my situation" can surely help you understand how this single word can affect your morale. Compare the aforementioned phrase with, "I'm going to put in my best effort and I'm going to improve my situation," or "I will work hard until things get better." This shows a subtle but powerful difference between the two mindsets. You adopt a reactive approach when you hope for things to happen. On the other hand, you act proactively when you take the right action and work for success. Get rid of the thought, "I hope things could work in my favor." Observe closely, and if you use the word hope in this context, interrupt yourself and say, "What measures could I take to make things work in my favor or to ensure my success?" The Old Phrase: I hope I get selected for the managerial position. The New Phrase: I am working hard to get selected for the managerial position. But This word has the power to refute everything that precedes it. For example, "I want to take a trip to the island but I don't have enough money." In this phrase, it sounds as if the individual will not go to the island. When a person hears the term "but", they automatically understand that they should disregard everything that was previously said. So what's the better way to convey the same message? Here you go: "I don't have enough money but I want to go to the island." Notice the difference? In this example, it seems as if the speaker will go to the island. Remember that "but" always disproves, so make sure to use it in the right manner if you have to use it. It is possible to convey the same message without using the word "but". You just have to substitute it with some other positive words. For instance, you can try using "and yet" to communicate the same thing. Try saying, "I want to go the island and yet I don't have enough money." The Old Phrase: I want to attend the seminar but I have many other assignments at the moment. The New Phrase: I want to attend the seminar and yet I have many other assignments at the moment. Wish Another word that you should eliminate to develop your vocabulary of confidence is "wish". Do you know what wishful thinking is? It is exactly the thing that does not let you move ahead. Have you ever noticed the associations this word builds in you? Throwing a coin into some fountain and expecting that it will fulfill your wish. This makes you wonder if it is possible to get the desired results with taking action. So remove this word immediately from your confidence vocabulary. The Old Phrase: I wish that I'd get top marks in exams. The New Phrase: I want top marks and I'm taking specific, massive, and effective steps to execute my study plan and get the desired marks in exams. Would/Should/Could These are usually considered interchangeable terms, but they all are not a good addition to your vocabulary. As we discuss each of these words, you'll see how their use can decrease your confidence. You'll also learn how you can replace them with better words that can propel you towards success. "Could" serves as an impediment to your success. If you see someone saying, "I could work on that project," ask him/her, "Then why don't you?" By using this word, you emphasize that a condition is associated with your action. I could set up and grow my business to new markets. I could make more people use my products. I could talk to strangers easily. "Could" presumes that some condition is stopping you from achieving all that. Get rid of it. The Old Phrase: I could try writing a crime novel for book lovers. The New Phrase: I can write a crime novel for book lovers. "Would" refers to some conditionality. You can't call it absolute. And that's why it takes confidence out of your conversation. When you use this term, you unconsciously give some reason to not pursue your dream. For instance, "I would go for that job interview and work for a big organization." This conditional "would" involves certain presumptions that something is stopping you from following your goals. So eliminate this word to add certainty to your conversation. The Old Phrase: I would go on the tour with you if only... The New Phrase: I will go on the tour with you. "Should" is the worst of these three terms. It indicates that there are some expectations involved and you don't have much choice in the selection of your behavior. Consider the sentence, "You should be working on this task right now." Ask yourself, you should be working on the given task according to whom? Whose expectations do you need to fulfill? The truth is your own expectations hold the maximum importance for you. After all, you need to lead your own life, make your own decisions. As a unique individual, you are in charge of your actions and behaviors. Using the term "should" is like making yourself a hostage and limiting your options. If you think that you should take certain actions in any situation, then you're not trying to explore other options. And this limiting perspective can become detrimental to your progress. The Old Phrase: It is getting dark and I should leave now. The New Phrase: It is getting dark so I choose to leave now.

Know the Confidence Boosters

After discussing the words that no confident person uses or should use, it's time to take a look at the words that not only signify a person's confidence but are also used to encourage others. As you make these words a definite part of your vocabulary, your thoughts, and speech, you adopt an effective approach to skyrocket your confidence. The fundamental principle is that these words depict your confidence and show that you know your aims and targets. The following list contains some of the best words that should be in your vocabulary to give you a great confidence boost: Positively Absolutely Definitely Undoubtedly Guaranteed Sure Naturally Obviously Of course Assuredly Certainly Without a question So how do these words work and create an impact on your thinking and personality? They basically convey a corresponding message like "this is how it is and I'm sure of it and I don't have any doubt in my mind about it." As you start using these words in your regular communication, your mindset and thinking pattern will change in the same way. What's more, you'll observe a change in the way people respond because your vocabulary will also have a positive impact on them. Let's say someone asks you, "What is it that you want to do?" What will be your response? "I don't know. I haven't thought about it. I'm not sure right now." "I certainly want to finish reading that book." Which of the two answers sound more confident to you? These simple examples are enough to show you the difference between a person who is confident and is ready to do something and a person who may want to achieve something but is too reluctant to say that.

7

Body Language Says it All

In order to have a magical body, you should have a magical mind first. Your internal feelings have a strong connection with your physiology. Some people move timidly or don't carry themselves with enough confidence. This causes them to feel less confident internally, and that is something that keeps them behind and less motivated. In stressful conditions, many individuals resort to placating and blaming. While doing this, they use particular gestures of blaming that make them go into the physical state of a lack of confidence. If they make efforts to change their attitude by maintaining confident physiology, they can have a control over their internal state and get it matched with that of a cool and calm person. As compared to placating and blaming, adopting a calm and cool behavior can prove to be a more effective approach to solve a problem. This section outlines a few useful methods that you can use to train your body to stay confident. The Walk Confident people's poise and coolness can be seen in the way they walk. This doesn't mean that you should walk pompously to let the world know that you are a confident person. Instead, you should have a certain cool and calmness to make your walk filled with confidence. If you see a confident person walking, you can feel them thinking, "I am absolutely successful and resourceful, because I don't doubt myself and I know that I can do things well." Practice walking like a confident person, and you'll eventually be able to project those positive, confident thoughts outward. As they become a part of your body language, you'll soon start observing some amazing changes in your overall personality. So what changes can you expect in your body language? Here are a few: with shoulders back, head held high, and tummy tucked in, you'll stand straight and move through the world with calculated, deliberate steps. And then you'll learn to walk at your own speed rather than trying to match the pace everyone else has. You won't find yourself constantly looking down at the ground, slouching, cracking your knuckles, or shuffling your feet. All in all, you'll notice many positive changes as you train your body to act confident. Gestures and Actions You might not see any confident person using placating gestures. After all, these gestures convey that the person making them is somehow submitting or inferior to others. Therefore, these gestures need to be avoided in all situations in order to build incredible confidence. A classic example of a wimpy gesture is that of a person shrugging his/her shoulders while having their palms faced upward. It seems as if they are supplicating, "I didn't know about it." This communicates that they are trying to make excuses and not taking the responsibility of a situation. Another example of a wimpy action is the shrug that indicates that people have no idea what is happening or perhaps they don't care. If you don't know something or have no idea what's going on, just let others know verbally in a clear, practical way. Individuals with a lack of confidence usually shrug in an evident way and convey in an annoyed or frustrated tone that they don't know anything. In most situations, it is possible for such people to find the right solution to their problems or queries if they just give it a thought instead of saying they have got no clue or blaming others. Confident people may not have the perfect answer immediately, but they know and understand that they have all the tools and resources to search and implement the solution. If someone asks you a question and your immediate response is, "I have no idea", or "I'm not sure how to go about it," this simply indicates to the other person that you are not even ready to think about it, to make an educated guess, or to look for an answer. So what's the better response in instances like these? If you really don't know the answer, it is always better to say, "I don't know yet." See the difference? This phrase lets the other person that you are uncertain right now, but you're willing to work for it and you might have an answer in the future. The opposite of wimpy gestures is blaming. Absolutely confident people never make a blaming gesture. And why would they? Such gestures simply mean that you are accusing others of something. People having the blame frame of mind don't empower those around them. If you see someone tightening up and pointing critically at others with their index finger, just know that they are simply declaring, "I've got nothing to do with it, it's all your fault." So how are confident people different from the ones who make such negative gestures? Well, confident people search for options to create solutions and resolve problems. They move through the world coolly, calmly, undisturbed by external events and conditions. The basic difference is that they keep a close check on their emotions, keep them controlled, and don't let them dominate them or destroy their personality. In order to behave like a confident person, you should avoid both wimpy and blaming gestures. Just be who you really are. An incredibly confident individual is the one who thinks outside the box to resolve problems and get the job done. They don't think about what or who caused something. Their main purpose is to find the solution and prevent the same problem from occurring again. Eye Contact Confident individuals can look others straight in the eye, and that's why they are perceived as being more genuine and sincere than a person who avoids direct eye contact. People with a lack of confidence are usually shifty-eyed. This makes others suspicious about their truthfulness and sincerity. If you don't have anything to hide, concentrate on looking at others directly in the eye. This will not only portray your confident image but will also make you feel good about yourself. If you're currently building your confidence and can't look at people in the eye, that's completely normal as a starting point. The following exercise can help you discover a natural and helpful way to do it. With this exercise, you can form the beginning of a positive habit. For this exercise, you need a supportive partner, such as a relative, friend, or spouse. Get a timer that can signal the end of 5 minutes. Sit across from the partner silently. Look straight in their eyes. While doing this exercise, you may have urges to look away or laugh. Just remember to perform the exercise with all your sincerity and continue to look at your partner in the eye. They'll do the same with you. If any of you laughs or looks away, just gently remind them to focus. Continue doing this exercise for 5 minutes. You can do it as many times as you want on a daily basis. Soon, you'll discover what it really feels like to maintain direct eye contact with someone. After doing this simple exercise, you can perform it in the real world and you'll be surprised to see how easy it is to communicate through eye contact. The Wonders of Touch Individuals with great confidence like to put other people at ease. They let others be comfortable in their presence. One method that they can use to relax others involves the magic of touch. Being touched is an amazing way to make a strong connection with other people. Whether the touch is an admiring pat on the back, a firm handshake, or a welcoming hug, people respond to friendly touch in a positive manner. Can you think of someone who is friendly and warm? Have you ever noticed how they behave with people? Chances are, they utilize the power of touch to create the human connection.

As you consider the usefulness of touch, you might come up with all of the various ways and contexts in which you can use it in your own daily life to boost your confidence. However, here's a word of warning for you. In the today's highly controversial environment of sexual harassment, you need to be extremely cautious of using the magic of touch. Make sure you understand how the other person may perceive your touch. So apply this method sensibly. The Smile If you want to portray yourself as a confident personality, smile. And for this purpose, smile at anyone and everyone, you come across. Do it when you are at home, at work, in the gym. No matter what you're doing, where you are, how you are feeling, just smile to make others as well as yourself feel good. Once you're expert at smiling, try making small talk. This will help you become more proficient at chatting and then you'll see that conversations can flow with great ease. If you're a naturally cheerful person, you won't find giving others the gift of a smile difficult at all. But if you're a shy individual who doesn't smile much, just practice it. And you'll notice pretty soon that people smile back at you when you smile at them. And this realization will give you a great confidence boost and urge you to continue this habit. Smile as much as you can because it is free and of course, very effective. What's more, people who smile naturally are usually perceived as more authentic, real, and trustworthy. So help others see your hidden traits with your smile. Interpersonal Skills A deep understanding of interpersonal skills can skyrocket your confidence. If you understand how individuals work, you are in a better position to get connected with them. Who is your best friend? Can you picture him/her in your mind? So what is it that you specifically like about them? Whatever characteristics you like about them, chances are that the following three characteristics make you attracted to them. The basis of most relationships are: Admiration Support Similarity Everyone likes to be admired. We want to be complimented for our accomplishments. Many times, employees become dissatisfied not because they don't get the right financial benefits, but instead because they are not rewarded with recognition. The next element to making a person like someone else is support. Without support, there is virtually no basis for any relation. People who support you, participate in different tasks with you, or help you out are usually more likable to you than someone who doesn't. Similarity is the final component that makes people like those who they think are like themselves. You may share a few common traits with your best friend. These may include anything from similar beliefs to dreams, hobbies, and to attitudes.

Understanding of similarity principle enables you to develop strong interpersonal relationships and develop personal confidence.

8
Creating a Bond Through Mirroring

If you create a connection with one or more individuals successfully, you just radiate confidence. As a result of this interesting connection, even your body physiology can get matched with them. It is then possible to use this bondage to your own benefit. You can further enhance your perceived connection with them by consciously matching their body language. This strategy is called mirroring as you try to become their mirror image. Many people confuse this technique with mimicking. However, the two strategies are based on completely different principles. While mimicking is something done to annoy others, mirroring helps increase the similarity between two or more people and ultimately stimulate a deeper understanding of their respective points of view. The latter is actually a respectful method you can use to understand people and their perspectives. The Mirroring Strategy The best way to mirror a person is to match their body posture. Move as they move. But make sure you do this while allowing for a particular lag time so your matching efforts don't creep them out. By lag time, we simply mean the duration it takes from their movement to your corresponding response. The basic idea here is to establish and then maintain a connection with them at an unconscious level. As your connection strengthens, you can reduce the lag duration until you move exactly with that individual. You can imagine connection as a dance where one person leads and the other follows. In the beginning of the mirroring strategy, you dance only as a follower. Once the connection is developed, you have an absolute opportunity to lead the dance. In order to lead, you need to bring your body into the position from where you can determine if the other individual is ready to follow you.

If you find them not following your movement for any reason, revert to mirroring and establish the connection further. Other than mirroring body language, it is also possible to mirror people's breathing patterns. Similar to body posture, this will unconsciously ensure a synchronized connection between you and the other individual. If you're ready to mirror someone's breathing, just observe their shoulders. After all, they rise when a person inhales and fall when they exhale. A good thing to remember while applying this strategy is that people usually exhale while talking. This piece of information will help you match a person's breathing. The more efficiently you mirror someone, the stronger connection you can establish with them. Matching someone's breathing is particularly easy if you are able to touch them. Let's say you try to synchronize with a friend or relative you are standing close to, it possible to actually feel their breaths as they breathe in and out. Just observe their inhale and exhale cycle, and then you can match them quite comfortably. Creating a Bond With Groups Since now you know how you can form a connection with others on a personal basis, it's time to find out if it is possible to create a bond with an entire group. Since it is extremely difficult to mirror every individual's vocal qualities and body language, the best strategy to create a bond with an entire group is to match the leader of the group. Regardless of the kind of group, there's always a leader. Discover who the group's leader is, establish a connection with them and that connection will then be transferred to the rest of the crowd. If you're not sure how to identify the group leader, ask loudly and clearly, "Why has the group assembled here today?" Everyone will turn and wait for the leader to respond. This will not only help you get the answer to your question but will enable you to identify the leader. From there, you can easily mirror the leader and build a bond with the entire group. Creating a Bond Nonverbally The following list highlights some of the most common nonverbal behaviors you can possibly match with other people: Body postures Facial expressions Hand gestures Muscle tension Breathing Eye blinks The extent of perceived connection between you and others is proportional to the strength of the bond you will create. The stronger bond you develop, the more confident you'll feel. The fundamental principle of mirroring is to do whatever they do. This might make you uncomfortable, but remember that you are deepening your connection so as to understand how they think. Mirroring makes you respectful to others. Getting your message across is your own responsibility. Make all possible efforts to fulfill this responsibility. Nonverbal mirroring can help you in this regard. In addition to matching someone's body breathing and body posture, you can mirror their hand gestures. Observe how people move their hands while talking. Try to match the other person's hand gestures no matter how wild, demonstrative, or precise they are. It might feel a bit awkward in the beginning, but constant practice will make you an expert. Match their hand movements to communicate with them in a better manner. Another nonverbal gesture that can help you develop a rapport with people is facial expression. Smile, raise of the eyebrow, frown, or other facial expressions can be mirrored. It is even possible to match the other person's muscle tone. If you think they are stressed out and tightened, you can tighten yourself up as well. If they are relaxed and loose, unwind yourself to match them perfectly. Suppose you're trying to build rapport with a person who is tensed. By creating a bond with them, you can lead them and help them gradually calm down. If the connection is strong, they'll not only follow you, but will also ultimately relax. In order to help someone change their emotional state, it is important to mirror their current emotional state, create a connection with them, and then make them follow you into a new, improved emotional state. This is the reason why most people get even angrier when they are advised in the calmest voice to relax. People who understand the mirroring strategy, on the other hand, will empathize with the other person using the same body language and tone to help them calm down. Creating a Bond Verbally Verbal behaviors can also help you deepen the bond with people. These behaviors typically include the rate at which people speak, voice tone, and vocabulary. If you're trying to create a connection with someone speaks very fast, it is better not to speak slowly to them. Keep up with their rate to match them. Similarly, don't speak rapidly if the other person speaks really slowly. It is essential to match the rate of their speech. If they use a few words a lot, it is most likely those words hold some importance to them. In order to establish the connection, try using those words in your conversation and discover the increased rapport. Pay attention to their key words that they use frequently. These words are often termed as trigger words. Use these words in all possible contexts and your connection will just skyrocket. The following list mentions a few verbal behaviors that you can match to maintain an improved rapport with others: Trigger words Volume of voice Vocal tone Rate at which they speak Inflection (commands, statements, questions) Pauses Gestures to Create a Bond As a skilled communicator, nod as you listen to others. By doing so, you can help them lessen their nervousness and share what they want to. If you want to practice this gesture, just seek a partner and converse with them. You don't need to say much, listen to them and nod frequently yet appropriately. This gesture creates a major difference between effective and disinterested communicators. Mirror effective communicators to build your confidence in interpersonal skills as well as your overall personality. Disinterested communicators can be easily identified by the way they slouch and lean back. Exceptional communicators, on the other hand, lean forward and show their interest in the other person's conversation. While performing the aforementioned exercise, make sure to lean a bit forward as you nod. Most confident individuals use a variety of words to keep other people talking and sharing whatever they have on their minds. Some of these words are mentioned below: Go on Uh-huh Really? Tell me more Sure That makes complete sense I know what you're trying to say I understand Mind Reading – Yes or No? Is mind reading a good idea to develop great confidence? While some people think this keeps them alert, others are of the opinion that this activity has a negative effect on their communication skills and interpersonal abilities. The truth is individuals who mind-read just pretend that they can read the other person's thoughts without communicating with them. This creates misunderstandings and problems among relations. What would you think of a friend who does not call you back? Do you get angry with a customer who does not contact you immediately? If you are involved in mind-reading, you would just assume that they betrayed you. However, if you believe in effective communication, you would understand that there can be many potential causes and the only efficient way to know is to call them up and ask. Observe yourself and determine if you just assume everything about others. If you do, ask yourself, "What makes me so sure? Did they say that? Can there be more explanations for their behavior?" Another negative aspect of mind reading is that such people just assume that others don't like them or don't want to be with them. This leads them to fear rejection and become shy. They are unable to interact with anyone because their shyness or nervousness incapacitates them. It is vital to practice and become more aware of yourself in order to figure out if you mind-read. Don't just automatically assume others' intentions and thoughts. Give them a chance to discuss and clarify their position. When you don't mind- read and actually communicate with people, not only you find it easier to talk to them, but they are also in a better position to open up with you. Give up mind reading to build incredible confidence.

9

internal voice

Your internal voice has a huge impact on your overall state of mind. You can speak to yourself in many ways, but not all can help you develop confidence. Imagine there's a stereo system in your mind that can play things that only you can hear. If it plays something in a droning, whining voice that constantly talks about your failures, you'd want to get rid of that playlist, wouldn't you? On the other hand, if it plays a warm, rich voice that reminds you of all your achievements, you'd feel great or even turn up the volume, right? This is how your internal voice alters your state of mind and drives your thoughts. In the next few sections, we'll be discussing how to train your internal voice to give you a confidence boost. Crush the Destructive Internal Thoughts Does your internal voice nag at you? Is it discouraging you from taking some step? Does it tell you that if you do something, you'd fail? Does it get louder every time you go outside your comfort zone? You need to stop this cycle of negative internal thoughts. Answer the questions below to identify the characteristics of internal dialogue. After all, once you know its specific qualities, you can take the right measures to silence it. Whose voice is it that criticizes you? Does the voice repeat its dialogues? Does it speak slowly or rapidly? What is its tone? In order to crush these destructive internal thoughts, just consciously change their qualities. For this, you can change the voice's vocal properties. For instance, imagine the same dialogues in the voice of Mickey Mouse or your favorite cartoon character. And then you might be amazed to see how easily an internal thought that used to disturb you becomes meaningless. Or speed up the voice such that it is almost incomprehensible. Imagine having a volume dial inside your mind to turn the internal thoughts' volume up or down as much as you want. Already feeling good knowing you have complete control over destructive internal thoughts? Just try this technique and enjoy the change. Amplify Constructive Internal Thoughts Just like you crush the destructive internal thoughts, do a few things to reinforce the positive internal dialogue. When you hear inspiring words inside your mind, stop doing everything and appreciate yourself. This will help you reinforce the behavior. Make sure your positive internal dialogue is in your own voice. The reason being only you can make your life's decisions. If that dialogue is in someone else's voice, you unconsciously hand over your power to them. Let those positive words resonate within you. Help them spread through your entire body. With the help of these constructive internal thoughts, you'll learn to trust yourself like any successful person. And then it won't matter if other people project their confines onto you. If someone gives you a bad advice or projects his/her boundaries onto you, just repeat the words "abandon, cancel" inside your mind. These words will flush out all negative thoughts and enable you to focus on positive, encouraging ideas. Quality Questions Lead to the Right Answers Your unconscious mind can answer almost any question for you. Therefore, it is vital to ask it the right questions so as to get the best answers. The better questions you ask, the better life you live. Many people, in an irritating muffled voice, ask themselves, "Why am I like this?" "Why don't I succeed?" Such depressing questions only emphasize one's stuck state of mind. Your unconscious mind will not only answer these horrible questions, but will also give you various reasons for your state of being stuck. Start asking yourself positive questions like, "How much can I achieve? How much can I enjoy? How great will it be to build more confidence? How amazing will I feel after overcoming this little fear?" When you ask such questions, your mind presumes that good things will happen eventually. As a result, it will search for answers and further help you get desired results. If you ask poor questions, your mind will reply with excuses and poor reasons for being stuck. If you ask great questions, it will give you every possible proof as to how amazing you are. Silence the Inner Critic So who is the inner critic and how does it work? Well, the inner critic is that evil little voice that occurs inside your head and constantly complains, condemns, and carps. It always sows doubt by saying, "Yes, but just suppose if you don't succeed in that. You know you will. It will not work. It never does." If you allow such negative thoughts to remain unchallenged, you, in a way, let the inner critic overpower you and damage your confidence. It is imperative to tell this voice to shut up and that it just needs to go away. Once you're able to get rid of this voice, you can work on your thoughts to make them more positive and helpful. This doesn't mean that you fear your negative thoughts. Instead, acknowledge what they are; just negative thoughts and not a representation of the truth. They don't deserve a space in your consciousness, so get rid of such false ideas and views as early as possible. Whenever such thoughts occur to you, ask yourself, "Why am I thinking like that? Will these thoughts help me gain confidence? Are they supporting my purpose?" These questions will help you realize that these thoughts are negative in nature, so you'll be better able to interrupt them. Just detach yourself from negative thoughts and think about something positive. You can shake your head, move your feet, slap your hand or do other such things to stop the thought. Another technique to achieve the purpose is saying particular words, such as no, go away, stop, or other phrases of your choice to yourself. Repeat these words aloud or silently as many times as you want to interrupt your thought process. Alternatively, have a good laugh at yourself and ponder over the absurdity of your negative thoughts. Imagine a cute, little figure is cleaning up the anxious, doubting, and useless thoughts inside your head. When they are all gathered up, blow the dust out of your mouth and see it scattering into your surroundings. Remind yourself that negative thoughts can't give you a hard time unless you allow them to do so.

10
Confidence Building Strategy

You just can't take negative thinking lightly as it can spiral out of control quite easily and quickly and then damage your confidence, without giving you any chance to work for its improvement. This is where you need special strategies to not only control, interrupt, or stop such thoughts, but also replace them with more helpful, positive ones. The strategy that we'll be discussing in this section is called The Four Step Strategy. This simple yet effective technique enables you to notice disempowering thought patterns. Once you become aware of these thoughts, you can prevent them from becoming a permanent part of your beliefs and views. You can easily learn and implement this strategy and make it your second nature. With this effective technique, you can develop great confidence and alter your life permanently for the better. Read on to discover the four steps that make up this strategy: 1. Practice Mindfulness By mindfulness, we simply mean that you pay special attention to what you think and feel. Be aware of the way you respond to people and different situations. As you become more attentive to these factors, your mind is better able to see and observe things more efficiently. You are then less likely to make hasty or illogical decisions. As a matter of fact, mindfulness improves your understanding of yourself and everything around you. It is the first step you can take towards the development of incredible confidence. 2. Stop Negative Thoughts Humans don't operate like robots. Though a bit difficult, it is possible to consciously decide how to think. If you really want to build your confidence, you need to start altering your thinking patterns immediately. Whenever you find yourself having negative thoughts, interrupt yourself and ask, "Am I thinking negatively again? Am I being a killjoy? Why do I find it so hard to think positively? Is my conversation often filled with doom and gloom?"

When answered truthfully, these questions can help you become aware of your true nature. Stop yourself at this point and make a conscious effort to avoid thinking negatively. 3. Replace Them With Positive Thoughts If the answers to all questions discussed in step 2 are yes, ask yourself, "What has my negative thoughts have given me so far? How confident would I be if I had more positive thoughts?" Figure out, and even write down, at least 5 differences that positive thinking pattern would make to your life. Learn to control and manage your thoughts so that you talk to yourself in an uplifting and positive fashion in all situations. Yes, it may require some practice, but it's definitely possible. Practice using sentences which start with positive phrases, such as "I do", "I choose", "I can", and "I am". 4. Continue Until it Becomes Your Nature Once you're able to identify, interrupt and replace your negative thoughts with the positive ones, make a promise to yourself that from this time forth you will never use discouraging terms, such as "I can't", I'm not sure", or "I'm unable". Make sure you never put yourself down. Remind yourself that everything is achievable; all you need is hard work. One of the most influential affirmations you can make is "YES". Say it frequently, enthusiastically. Whenever you find a new opportunity, say to yourself that you can make everything possible. Accept every challenge or problem and put in your best effort to make it work.

11

Basics to Develop Unrelenting Confidence

you have now reached the stage where you're ready to work on your own confidence building strategy. So how can you develop this acute sense of balanced confidence, based on a strong appreciation of reality? The truth is there's no quick fix involved. However, it is possible to gain unstoppable confidence if you have the determination and focus on getting through. Another amazing thing you should know is that the strategies you use to build confidence will also help you achieve success. After all, confidence originates from real achievements. And no one has the power to take that away from you. So read on and find your way to building irreplaceable confidence. Step I: Prepare for the Journey The first and the most important step to develop confidence is to get yourself prepared for the upcoming journey. In this step, take note of your current position, determine what you want to achieve, check your mindset, and make a commitment to complete the journey no matter what. Let's take a quick look at each of these steps. Identify Your Current State Think about your life, things that matter to you, and what you want to accomplish in the future. Defining and accomplishing goals is an important part of this journey. This is where real confidence comes from. Use the process of goal setting to make achievable targets and then measure your successful realization of those goals. Identify Your Achievements Think about your life in general and list down some of your best achievements in a "Success Chart". Perhaps you got the top score in an exam, played a lead role in your school play, scored a match-winning goal, produced great sales figures, helped someone out, or completed a project ahead of schedule. Put all such achievements into a neatly formatted document so that you can check it when you want. Spend some minutes every week going through this chart to take pleasure in the achievements you've made in your life so far. Identify Your Resources Next, try to explore your hidden strengths and your current position in life. Observe your success chart carefully, reflect on your current life, and try to determine what your friends or family would think your strengths and weaknesses are. Afterward, dwell on the opportunities and threats that you might have to face on the way. Don't forget to take some time to enjoy your strengths. Identify the Future YOU Imagine that your future self has unlimited confidence as compared to your current self. Try to picture how he/she speaks, talks, walks, moves, gestures, and does everything in general. Observe it. Hear through its ears. See through its eyes. Feel what happens when you project unstoppable confidence. The part step of this preparation is to make a clear promise to yourself that you will complete the journey and do everything possible to achieve that ultimate confidence. Step II: Set Out for the Journey This is the phase where you actually start working toward your goal. Begin with easy, small achievements and continue your journey on the path to success. Rectify Past Mistakes Go back into the past when you did something wrong. Perhaps you didn't make the right effort or did something that just took success away from you. Go back to the time when you deviated from your success path, and replace the original ending with your desired ending. You'll observe how things appear and feel different. Since your past has improved, you'll find yourself moving through the world more confidently. Define Your Goals and Schedule Them Start with small, simple goals you identified in the previous step. Make a habit of setting, achieving, and celebrating your goals. Avoid making challenging goals at this stage as it will make it difficult for you to move on. And then pile up the successes. An important thing to remember at this stage is that goals are most effective when they have deadlines. Imagine yourself five or so years into the future leading your dream lifestyle. What have you achieved? How is your home like? What organization do you work for? Focus on the answers to these questions and then jot down the skills and accomplishments you want in the future. Borrow Confidence Next, gain confidence from someone who you think has high confidence levels. Determine how they make their way through the world as meticulously as possible. Get to know them closely or spend time with them. The key here is to get your mind connected with them as much as possible. The better you understand their values, attitudes, and beliefs, the more efficiently you can borrow confidence from them. Step III: Accelerate Toward Success By this phase, you'll feel your confidence developing. You can now stretch yourself. Set bigger, more complex goals. Diversify your commitments. Extend your skills. Meet Your Confident Clone And this is when you meet your new confident self. By this stage, you are ready to do things differently, accept new challenges, and interact with almost anyone. You as well as others can notice a positive difference in your walk, style, gestures, and personality. After all, every aspect of your personality now projects unlimited confidence.

12
Reminders to Develop Ultimate Confidence

Getting started on the development of confidence may be the most difficult part for you, so you are advised to use the tips discussed in this section to turn things around. Just put in the effort, and you will soon feel a positive change. We all have confidence within us, but sometimes, it can get lost as the world throws us constant curveballs. Spend some days working on a single tip that works for you, and then implement another. This will help you feel more confident and better about your life. Learn how to restructure your confidence; it is important to living a satisfied life. Situations that make us doubt whether we are capable enough will come along; when this happens, these tips will help you get back on track and resume your confidence building journey. The following tools can give you the confidence you need in difficult times, so try using these whenever you find yourself losing confidence. Confidence can be Developed You need to understand that confidence is not something that you cannot acquire. However, if not acquired successfully, its absence can hamper your growth and progress. Persistence and never-ending desire are the basic elements that can keep you motivated toward your goal. You can grow and succeed only when you are able to think, dream, and contemplate. Your reflections, ideas, and thoughts can boost your confidence, but you have to recognize their value so as to get maximize their full potential. Find What Lies Within It is important to discover the confidence that is hidden somewhere within you. Realizing that you are a person of integrity and honor can keep you on a positive and purposeful path. Another fact that might help you continue your journey is that people with a solid moral fiber are usually more confident people. So try to be more honest and truthful to develop and maintain great confidence. Do Something Good for Others Supporting others enables you to understand that you are a good individual who can utilize your knowledge, skills, and abilities in a positive, helpful manner. Also, you will get a priceless feeling by giving something to those who are less fortunate than you. Practice "As if" Live the life as if it is already giving you everything good. This can serve as an amazing psychological tool for developing confidence. By practicing and implementing this valuable tool, you can learn to emotionally and physically feel success. Moreover, you send a positive, encouraging vibe to others that can surely keep them motivated as well. Work With a Mentor If your parents were not supportive enough or couldn't help you build selfconfidence during your childhood days, it's not too late. You can find someone in the field you love or you respect and ask him/her to become your mentor. To tell you the truth, most individuals are flattered by such requests and do everything possible to help others out.

Look After Yourself Eat healthy, work on your energy levels, lead an active lifestyle, participate in physical activities, exercise or work out, and give yourself special rewards for all your accomplishments. Always remember a physically and emotionally healthy person can achieve almost anything. If you are not one of those individuals, mere survival can become a great challenge for you. Being healthy and active is vital to not only your physical well-being but also your confidence. Do you know what's the easiest, most economical and effective kind of antidepressant? The answer is exercise. So instead of just sitting there on the sofa, watching TV, using mind-numbing apps on your cellphone, or working on your computer for unlimited hours, go out and see it's a wonderful day to jog, run, cycle, and help your mind and body recover. Get up and get busy. Experience If you've been there once, you can go there again and again. Even if it happened many years ago, most things are like riding a bicycle. Like most individuals, you may be unable to balance yourself when you initially try again, but the skill returns quickly. Always remember that knowledge gives you power. If you make a constant effort to actually learn what is being taught to you, then you can never get off track.

Maintain a Confidence Log This technique is simple, easy, and rejuvenating for both your mind and emotions. Just list down five or six things you think you are confident about. Do it on a daily basis, and soon you'll have a journal highlighting both the positive and negative changes in your thinking and feelings. So what's the best time to write the confidence log? Right before going to bed. This is the time when gratefulness can flow into your subconscious. What's more, this small activity can help you wake up a little more confident and of course, happy about your life. Create a Support Structure Support groups are not a new concept. Then have been in use much longer than psychoanalysis. Back in the old days, people related to the field of medicine would gather to share their tools and techniques and individuals could seek out their help. Apply the same concept to boost your confidence. Seek help from supportive family members, friends, colleagues, etc. If they can't offer you the help you're looking for, you can also join a group. Alternatively, create a support group of your own and help others as well.

Monitor Your Thoughts According to some researches, out of the innumerable thoughts we have during an entire day, nearly 80 percent are destructive. They further inform us that our mind is designed to remember the destructive thoughts because that is how we are created. Times are changing now, so our thinking process should change as well. Reflect on positive thoughts consciously. Persevere until it becomes your second nature.

Do Not Discount Yourself There are some psychological researches that connect this form of thinking to poor self-esteem and depression. The less you appreciate what you do or achieve, the more you pull yourself down. Negative thinking is the basic element of depression. According to cognitive-behavioral analysts, if you wish to feel inadequate, depressed, and worthless, all you need to do is think in negative terms about yourself and your abilities. Identify your personal value and appreciate yourself for everything you do. Don't say things like, "Others are better than me" or "that doesn't matter". Praise yourself the way your friends would do. Appreciate Life List down three things that you are happy about at the end of your day along with the reasons why they make you happy to notice significant improvements in your moods in just two weeks. The benefits of this simple exercise can be enjoyed even after months. So get a journal or diary and start creating a list of things that make you happy. And you'll be surprised to see many small things that you usually don't notice much in that list. This exercise will help you realize that it is sometimes the small things in life that enable you to develop confidence and improve your capability to feel gratitude. Look Good to Feel Good Go visit your regular salon and get a makeover. No, you don't need to spend hefty amounts to do this. You can even go to a charity shop in a residential area and find quality designer clothes and many other accessories at affordable rates. Gather information about your nearest beauty and hairdressing training schools as they are often searching for models. You can offer to serve as their model and pay just a small amount to get your hair done. Get an affordable personal shopper as they can help you shop for suitable clothes and. These people are trained to see the beauty in us that we often overlook ourselves. Is your birthday coming up? Make a suggestion to your friends and family and encourage them to donate towards your makeover fund. Change the way you look to gain better confidence. This will make you feel good and see the world in a different manner. Accept Challenges Confident individuals take risks and handle them well. Make these risks work in your favor. If you think you can achieve something, then you certainly can. If you pretend to become confident, then you have better chances to actually become confident. If you have to go to a party or social event, think about all the confident people you know and their behavior. How do they move? How do they talk? How do they behave with others? If you can, observe them in action. You can even note down all the things they do. Afterwards, practice them. This strategy is referred to as modeling. Many successful and confident individuals do it unconsciously. You might feel uncomfortable at first but continue practicing, and soon you'll feel as if it has always been your natural behavior. Whether you are thin, fat, short, or tall, always remember that people get attracted to those who seem approachable and welcoming. Act as if you are this kind of person, and you'll see how many friends you make. You'll feel good about yourself. Part Thirteen: Confidence Building Activities Not having confidence in your abilities is an extremely harmful characteristic that can have severe consequences. Such people may not be able to stand up for themselves or take critical decisions, experience depression or frustration, become a naysayer, enter into damaging relationships, or may just not grow or progress. For them, it is significantly important to build their confidence, respect themselves, and realize their worth so as to succeed in life. Everyone at some point in their live feels insecure about themselves, lack the confidence to utilize their abilities and talents, or have disempowering thoughts. Nevertheless, if you think that is how you feel most of the time and it affects your daily life negatively, then the activities discussed in this section may help you out. Practice these activities as often as you want to notice a significant change in your confidence level. The best thing is these activities don't follow any chronological order, so you can utilize them interchangeably as well as simultaneously. After all, only you can decide which activity works best for you and gives you the desired results. Whether you want to perform these exercised in a group or on your own, the choice is completely yours. What Does the Name Denote? This is a helpful activity that can help people boosting their self-confidence. It is better to perform this exercise in a group or with your friends. Give a piece of paper to each group member. Make them write their name in big font so each letter is some distance apart. They can even write their name vertically. Once all have written their names, ask them to fold the paper and put it in a box. Mix them well. Distribute them randomly so no person gets the paper with his/her own name. Ask group members to think of a positive trait of the individual - whose name is given on the paper – that begins with each letter of the name. For instance, if the paper has the name "ADAM", positive qualities can be something like A – Attentive, D – Daring, A – Adventurous, M – Motivated. Once everyone has written all qualities, ask them stand up and read them aloud. This activity will let every individual realize the qualities that they might not have noticed about themselves before. Develop the Line of Pride Pride is associated with self-concept. Most people like expressing pride in the things they did but couldn't be recognized. Many cultures don't appreciate such expressions and that's why it becomes difficult for many people to actually state, "I'm proud of my ability to..." In this exercise, you, while working with your mentor or in a support group, express your pride about a particular area of behavior. Begin your statement with, "I'm proud (of my/that I/ because...". Following are a few topics you can use to discuss your pride: Work in office/school Things you did for your parents Things you did for your friends Things you did for your colleagues Something you have bought lately Something that you frequently do Something you shared with those inferior to you Something you worked hard for Your views about those who are different from you How you made some money Good, healthy habits The Gift This interesting activity is best played when all group members know each other. Divide group members into pairs. Give each member a chart paper. Since they all know each other, they are asked to think of a perfect gift for their partners considering their likes and dislikes. Every member has to draw the gift on the chart paper. Once they are done, ask them individually to show their artwork to the entire group and tell the reason why they choose a particular gift. This fun game helps to create a bond. Moreover, each member feels appreciated and a little more confident. Picture Yourself This is a great confidence building activity for almost any age level. However, its overall duration depends on the overall age level and the kind of medium selected. Create a self-portrait impromptu either from a mirror or from memory. You can sketch, paint or even draw. A vast variety of media, including chalk, ink, pencil, crayon, charcoal, tempera, pastel, or watercolor can be used for this purpose. Be accepting to your initial try. Try again after a few weeks. You can even get feedback on your portrait from a friend or someone who you respect. Display the self-portraits often on special occasions, such as birthdays, family dinners, anniversaries, etc. The Mirror Exercise In this activity, you can reveal and discover many positive things about yourself. Sit or stand in front of a mirror for a minute and think about things that you like about yourself. These things can be related to your physique, personality, abilities, skills, relationships, appearance, or anything at all. Say all the things that make you feel good about yourself loudly. You can ask a friend or family member to note down the things you say. Review this list later to see the strengths and aspirations that you never noticed before. Knowing Yourself Self-acceptance is the stage in the process of self-discovery that a person reaches only when they scrutinize their nature, personality, and traits objectively. On doing so, they understand that their strengths are far greater and better than their weaknesses. Take a look at the following questions and answer them truthfully. With this exercise, you can validate your positive self-perception. 1. List three things that you like about yourself. 2. List your top three strengths. 3. Give three reasons why it is important for you to build confidence. 4. List three incidents when lack of confidence had an impact on your life. 5. List three activities that, in your opinion, can make you a stronger and better person. Have a Dialogue Perform this exercise with your mentor or friend who you can easily talk to. Choose any of the following conversation topics to express your opinions. Comment on every question. Your mentor or friend can use your answers for further discussion. Describe yourself as a stranger might see you. Describe yourself as a friend or relative might see you. What is the most important lesson you've learned so far? What is the perfect job for a youngster? Why should a person be trusted? Describe the characteristics you admire in a person. When have you been blamed for something that you didn't do? How do you show your anger? Ten Things Ten Things is another helpful confidence building activity that should be performed in a group. Divide the group members into pairs. Ask every member to observe his/her partner for five minutes. When the time is over, ask them to list down ten things they like about their partner. You can even extend the activity by asking group members to also list down ten things they don't like about their partner. This extension works well when partners know each other well. With this exercise, you can understand how your first impression goes. Doer or Not? So who is a doer? A doer is someone who enjoys working outdoors with animals and plants, who plays with tools, or who is athletic or action-oriented. Answer the following questions to determine whether or not you are a doer. Once answered, use your responses to figure out how you can improve your weak aspects. Do you enjoy being outdoors? Do you like to work with tools and equipment? Have you ever taken apart and then reassembled mechanical equipment? Do you like animals or plants? Which would you prefer: working at a comfortable desk or physical activity? Do you play sports? Is physical fitness important to you? Are you a quick learner? Can you work in teams or groups? Can you understand processes from drawings and pictures? Flip-Flop Perform this activity in a group. Divide group members into pairs. Give a piece of paper to each member. Ask every member to list ten positive things and five negative things about themselves. These things can be related to their appearance, health, skills, emotions, or anything else. Once they are finished writing, ask them to give their sheet to their partner. Ask the partner to read the things mentioned in the list. They also have to give solutions or advice about the five negative things in order to convert them into positive qualities. This exercise provides a person with a healthy perspective as well as a solution to improve his/her personality.

Gratitude Rehearsal People who practice appreciation and thankfulness have lower levels of stress and depression. They are content with their relationships. Also, they enjoy longlasting positive effects. A few recommended activities for gratitude rehearsal include writing an appreciation letter and thanking someone important. Think about a person who has played a positive role in your personal or professional development, has done something good for you, or whom you would like to appreciate for his/her efforts. Write an appreciation letter with explicit details about the things you want to appreciate about them. Send it. Positive Experience Identification In this exercise, make conscious efforts to identify situations when you displayed different positive characteristics. Write about a time when you showed kindness, courage, selflessness, wisdom, determination, sacrifice, love, and happiness. By thinking about these experiences, you'll be better able to remind yourself that you still have the potential to be productive and confident. Presenting Life Story This exercise is a blend of positive psychology and narrative art. While performing this activity, you write your life story in 3 different parts, including the past, present, and future. Presenting Life Story can basically help you build a sense of purpose that can further contribute to your satisfaction. Be creative, but make sure you identify your personal strengths in every section. In the past section, describe all the challenges you overcame and the strengths that played a pivotal role. In the present section, describe your current life and explain how it is different from your past. In the last part, discuss how you visualize your ideal future and how you intend to achieve it. Strength Identification People having low confidence levels often find it difficult to think about their positive qualities. However, with some support, they can certainly come up with many ideas. This exercise can help you create a better image of yourself. Complete the worksheet involved in this activity and review it on a daily basis to remember your strengths and positive traits. Write at least three statements for each point: Compliments people have given me: Things I am better at: Things I like about my appearance: Challenge I have overcome successfully: Things that make me different from others: Things that others thank me for: When I made others happy: When I helped others: Encountering Negative Thoughts Challenge your negative thoughts using this exercise. Answer the following questions to evaluate your thought more objectively. Do you have any evidence for your thought? Do you have any evidence contrary to your thought? Do you have enough evidence to interpret the situation? How would a friend respond to this situation.

www.ingramcontent.com/pod-product-compliance
Lightning Source LLC
Chambersburg PA
CBHW061642130726
47996CB00003B/1422